Executive Summary

The purpose of this white paper is to describe a proposed framework for both a new securitization platform and a model Pooling and Servicing Agreement as set forth in the February 2012 *Strategic Plan for Enterprise Conservatorships* (Strategic Plan) published by the Federal Housing Finance Agency (FHFA). The Strategic Plan envisions the building and use of a new infrastructure by Fannie Mae and Freddie Mac (the Enterprises) as an efficient, logical extension of existing FHFA initiatives aligning the standards and practices of the Enterprises. It also envisions that this effort could have broader application to the future housing finance market.

The proposed infrastructure has two complementary goals: (1) replace the outmoded proprietary infrastructures of the Enterprises with a common, more efficient model; and (2) establish a framework that is consistent with multiple states of housing finance reform, including greater participation of private capital in assuming credit risk. Success in achieving these goals will provide a sound, efficient and flexible operating environment in the shorter term, and help provide policy makers with the means to design a mortgage finance system unfettered by legacy processes and systems and capable of working well with or without various degrees of government involvement.

Section 1, frames this project in both regulatory and market terms. In Section 2, we (FHFA and the Enterprises) set the context by describing the existing securitization models: Enterprise, Government National Mortgage Association (Ginnie Mae) and Private Label. Section 3 sets forth the proposed framework itself, with Part 3A describing the platform and its functions, and Part 3B describing the legal agreements, rules and responsibilities critical to the infrastructure as an integrated whole.

Part 3A explores common forms of credit enhancement – insurance and subordination – and outlines probable paths for private institutions that choose to make use of the new securitization infrastructure. The paper focuses on the infrastructure's scope; which includes the issuance of securities, as well as the accompanying disclosures, payments to investors, and dissemination of data on an ongoing basis; and presents the key principles for the needed software: open architecture, standard interfaces, data transparency and straight-through processing. Part 3A ends with the requirement of platform interoperability, proposing a service integration approach that should be accommodating to any issuer, Enterprise, servicer, agent or other counterparty that decides to participate.

Part 3B describes a framework for a model Pooling and Servicing Agreement, using preferred features from Enterprise, Ginnie Mae and private sector experience. We suggest that the model Pooling and Servicing Agreement be shorter, more flexible and more transparent than those that prevailed during the housing bubble. The model Pooling and Servicing Agreement could have selling and servicing standards similar to those used by the Enterprises to provide for the adoption of preferred practices throughout the life of a security, as well as the standardization and robust data necessary for the efficient functioning of a viable secondary market.

Section 4 addresses policy and regulatory considerations, recognizing much uncertainty remains. Finally, we ask for public input on both the securitization platform and model Pooling and Servicing Agreement and set forth some specific questions on which we hope to obtain thoughtful views.

1) Introduction

FHFA released to Congress the *Strategic Plan for Enterprise Conservatorships* in February 2012. As Acting Director Edward DeMarco noted "…FHFA is contemplating next steps to build an infrastructure for the secondary mortgage market that is consistent with existing policy proposals and will support any outcome of the leading legislative proposals." The plan sets forth three strategic goals for the next phase of the conservatorships:

1. *Build.* Build a new infrastructure for the secondary mortgage market.
2. *Contract.* Gradually contract the Enterprises' dominant presence in the marketplace while simplifying and shrinking their operations.
3. *Maintain.* Maintain foreclosure prevention activities and credit availability for new and refinanced mortgages.

The effort to create a new infrastructure for the secondary mortgage market connects all three of these goals. To maintain the efficient flow of mortgage credit, the existing antiquated and inflexible Enterprise infrastructures must be upgraded. In addition, a transition to a future securitization framework would require a more flexible infrastructure than currently available to accommodate future policy decisions. Given that the expenditures for the upgrades are necessary, it makes sense to direct them toward the development of a common flexible infrastructure for the two Enterprises to accommodate various securitization structures and policy goals. The discussion below addresses important elements of both a common securitization platform as well as a framework for a model Pooling and Servicing Agreement (PSA). It is intended to establish an open exchange of ideas with the industry that will foster and facilitate the further development of these concepts.

As noted in the Strategic Plan, the absence of any meaningful secondary mortgage market mechanisms beyond the Enterprises and the Government National Mortgage Association impedes the transition to a post-conservatorship secondary mortgage market. However, there are certain elements for rebuilding the housing finance system that are needed regardless of its ultimate structure. In particular, a future housing finance system needs an operational mechanism that connects capital market investors to borrowers by bundling mortgages into securities and tracking payments (referred to in this paper as the securitization platform). A future housing finance system also needs rules for certain key functions. Specifically, it would be useful to have a standardized model PSA that replaces parts of the Enterprises' contractual architecture and that addresses shortcomings found in Private Label agreements.

FHFA believes work can begin on these two cornerstone elements even in the absence of certainty regarding the ultimate housing finance structure and presence of a government guarantee in the future. In essence, FHFA proposes a structure that follows an incremental approach to building a securitization infrastructure for the future, starting with the very basic elements and enhancing the scope with feedback from the industry and other regulatory agencies and decisions from policymakers.

At present, approximately 75 percent of mortgage securitization is performed by the two Enterprises in conservatorship while roughly 25 percent is performed by Ginnie Mae. Two key goals of this proposal are to continue the availability of mortgage funding (i.e. provide liquidity) and to develop a framework that can serve the needs of a future housing finance system, including the entry of private capital in credit risk taking.

There are some core functionalities of a securitization infrastructure that can be standardized and serve a utility function. These functions fall under the headings of issuance, master servicing, bond administration, collateral management and data integration. As we plan the inclusion of various functions in the securitization platform and the model PSA, we would focus on those core functions that would provide a foundation for the overall infrastructure. Mortgage securitization encompasses a broad spectrum of stakeholders from borrowers, through a host of intermediaries such as originators/lenders, securitizers/issuers, trustees and bond administrators, and finally to investors. Securitization is also subject to oversight by a range of regulatory agencies and compliance with existing and proposed rules and regulations. In directing the Enterprises to begin work, FHFA is mindful of the role of other stakeholders. The securitization platform must be flexible enough to adapt to the evolving standards and requirements of other regulatory agencies as well as the future direction provided by Congress. To achieve these goals, FHFA provided direction to the Enterprises in the form of the 2012 Conservatorship Scorecards. Included in that Scorecard are the following requirements:

- Securitization Platform: FHFA and the Enterprises will collaborate to "…develop and finalize a plan by December 31, 2012 for the design and build of a single securitization platform that can serve both Enterprises and a post-conservatorship market with multiple future issuers"

- Model PSA: FHFA and the Enterprises will collaborate to "Propose a model pooling and servicing agreement (PSA), seek public comment, and produce final recommendations for standard Enterprise trust documentation by December 31, 2012."

The goal in designing the common securitization platform and model PSA is to help streamline and simplify those functions that are commoditized and routinely repeated across the secondary mortgage market. FHFA believes that the design principles discussed in this paper provide a strong foundation to align and standardize existing practices, enhance the ability to attract private capital for credit risk and accommodate many future housing finance models.

2) Current State of Securitization Infrastructures

The current state of the mortgage secondary market consists of three models for securities issuance: Enterprise, Ginnie Mae and Private Label. After the global financial crisis of 2008, Private Label issuance shrank dramatically, while Enterprise and Ginnie Mae issuance filled the void and dominated the market. This has resulted in the government supporting the vast majority of newly originated mortgages. While the Enterprises and Ginnie Mae have standardized PSAs, the Private Label market is characterized by customized, non-standard agreements. Below is a brief description of the existing platforms.

A) Current Platforms

Enterprise Platforms

In the current market, the Enterprises perform many different securitization functions which include: issuance, trustee, guarantee, credit underwriting and pricing, master servicing, and credit loss management. While the requirements of the Enterprises are substantially similar, and recent joint initiatives are driving alignment in servicing standards, delivery data requirements, representations and warranty requirements and securities disclosures; the separate Enterprise infrastructures force market participants (such as sellers, servicers, and investors) to manage two distinct processes. Additionally, each Enterprise continues to make separate investments in maintaining its set of guides and contractual framework, increasing the cost to taxpayers during conservatorship. Channeling resources into a common securitization platform alleviates the need to make duplicate investments to maintain and upgrade two separate platforms currently being managed by the Enterprises to support their high volumes of securitization.

Figure 1 identifies in white the functions of the existing housing finance market that are within the scope of the current Enterprise business model.

Figure 1: Enterprise Scope

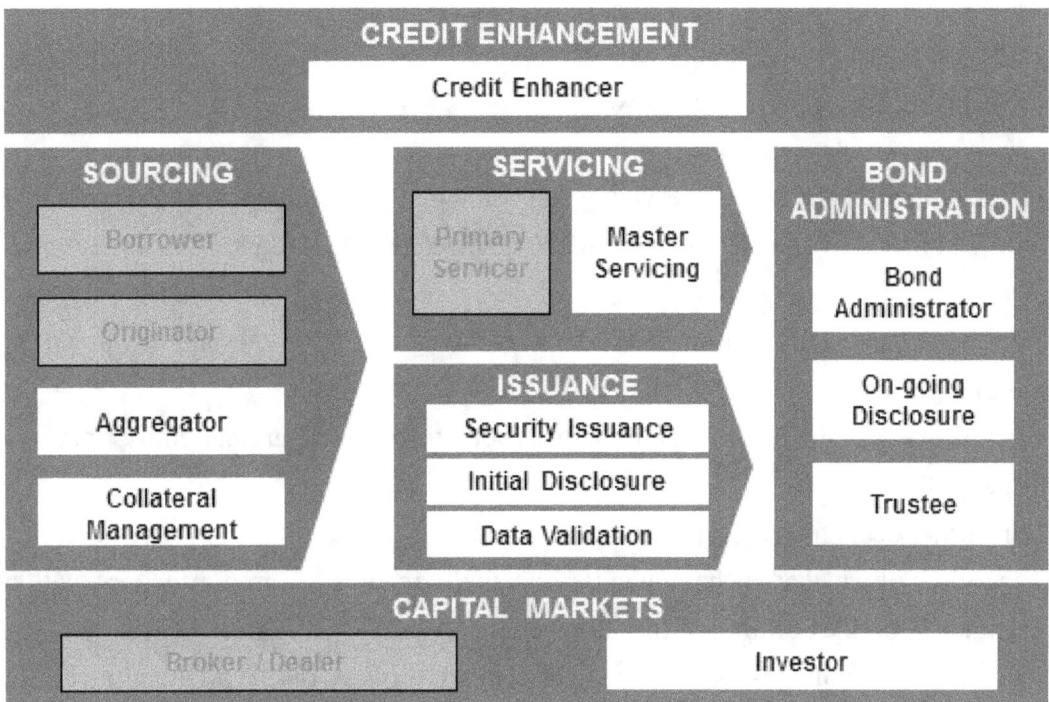

- Credit Enhancement – provides guarantee against credit-related loss.
- Sourcing – aggregates loans; manages and tracks assignment of mortgage notes.
- Servicing – performs master servicing; manages asset and cash activities; interfaces to servicers, guarantors, and aggregators.
- Issuance – prepares and issues securities in accordance with standard security, pooling and trust contracts.
- Bond administration – produces investor and third party disclosures; distributes principal and interest; monitors securities; addresses servicer shortfall; produces portfolio reporting.
- Capital Markets – provides capital to fund securitization process.

Ginnie Mae Platform

By contrast, Ginnie Mae's mandate is to administer the mortgage-backed securities program under which federally insured residential mortgage loans are securitized. Under the program, participating lenders and servicers (issuers) pool loans that have been insured or guaranteed under programs sponsored by Federal Housing Administration (FHA), US Department of Veterans Affairs (VA) and the US Department of Agriculture (USDA). The pooled loans are issued as securities by the issuers, not Ginnie Mae. Issuers assume full responsibility for remitting the contractual payments to which the security holders are entitled. Key differences in attributes of the Ginnie Mae model from the Enterprises may be divided into two broad categories: 1) Credit Exposure, and 2) Infrastructure.

Credit Exposure: From a credit perspective the Ginnie Mae program differs from those of the Enterprises in several important ways:

1) The origination and default servicing standards that govern the loans in Ginnie Mae pools are established by the sponsoring federal agencies (FHA, VA and USDA), not by Ginnie Mae.
2) The credit risk resulting from the loans is borne by these agencies and the issuer, not Ginnie Mae.
3) The securities are issued by the issuer (participating lender/servicer entity), not by Ginnie Mae.
4) The issuer bears full responsibility for remittance of payments to security holders, regardless of whether such payments are actually received from mortgagors, with no limitations on the duration of this advancing.
5) Ginnie Mae mainly has exposure to servicer counterparty risk, while the Enterprises also have exposure to mortgage insurers and borrowers.

Infrastructure: Figure 2 identifies in white the functions of the current housing finance market that are within the scope of the Ginnie Mae business model. The securitization platform in the Ginnie Mae model comprises the same elements as those of the Enterprises. However, Ginnie Mae is directly responsible for fewer of those functions, using an outsourcing model to manage its business. Ginnie Mae reserves for itself policy-making, management of contract and non-contract resources, risk management and relationship management functions, but most other functions are handled by third parties. Unlike the Enterprises, which issue their own securities, in the Ginnie Mae model the lender is responsible for issuance. Since loan level credit analysis is handled by the FHA, VA, and USDA, not Ginnie Mae, their model necessitates fewer operational functions, since Ginnie Mae has less concern with loan level credit, market transactions, portfolio management hedging and other functions that are not required by its role as a guarantor. Ginnie Mae works with third parties to manage its master servicing and bond administration functions, but does not perform all of the functionality executed in the Enterprise model.

Figure 2: Ginnie Mae Scope

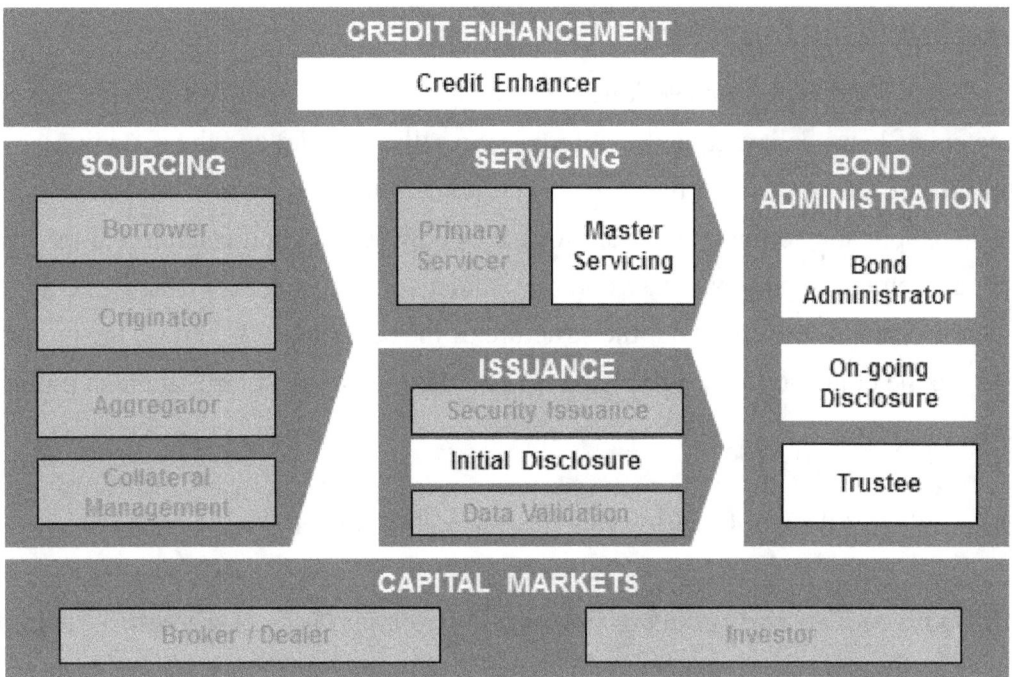

It is important to note that Ginnie Mae works with experienced service providers and all key decisions and judgments with regard to the various outsourced functions are retained by Ginnie Mae. In comparison, the Enterprise model is analogous to the combined roles of the FHA/VA as loan insurer or guarantor, the seller/servicer as issuer, and Ginnie Mae as security guarantor.

Private Label Securities Platforms

The Private Label Securities (PLS) market relies on private investment capital to support the market with private parties performing all the functions shown above. Credit risk is either retained by the aggregator or investor, guaranteed by a third party or re-packaged into new securitization structures. PLS market participants rely more on customizing their own rules for underwriting, pooling and servicing than in the existing Enterprise model. The PLS market was extremely active from 2004-2007. However, since the financial crisis began, PLS activity has been severely limited as investors have generally avoided mortgage credit risk. There has been some recent activity in this market but there does not yet appear to be a significant amount of private capital to provide mortgage credit in scale. Private Label securitizations rely solely on private capital and do not require a government guarantee.

B) Current Legal Contractual Framework and PSAs

Enterprise Contractual Framework

The current legal document framework used by each Enterprise consists of a guide that sets forth the parameters of loans delivered to the Enterprise (a selling guide) and the servicing responsibilities of the servicers of the loans (a servicing guide), an agreement that prescribes general terms applicable to the transfer of mortgages between a specific seller and the Enterprise (the master agreement or pool purchase contract) and a very short master trust agreement and series-specific supplement setting out the structure of the securities. Together, the guides and the documents are the equivalent of a Private Label PSA and its related mortgage loan purchase agreement.

A brief description of the key Enterprise documents includes:

> ***Mortgage Selling and Servicing Contract Agreement (Sales Agreement)*** - Establishes basic contractual requirements to do business with the Enterprise - whole loan or mortgage-backed securities (MBS). Single agreement signed by all lenders.
>
> ***Selling Guide*** - Outlines the guidelines for selling to the Enterprises and identifies the representations and warranties concerning the lender and the mortgage loans.
>
> ***Servicing Guide*** - Covers standard requirements for servicing Enterprise mortgages.
>
> ***MBS Purchase Agreement (Purchase Agreement)*** - Lender specific contracts that establish individual lender requirements, pricing, product eligibility and variances.
>
> ***Master Trust Agreement*** - Establishes the rights of certificate holders and the legal responsibilities of the Enterprise as Issuer, Master Servicer, Trustee and Guarantor.
>
> ***Issue Supplement to the Master Trust Agreement*** - A system generated document that evidences the delivery of a particular pool of loans into the related trust. There is an Issue Supplement for each MBS and Participation Certificate (PC) issued.
>
> ***Master Custodial Agreement*** - Identifies the document custodian that the lender has selected for all loans delivered to the Enterprise.
>
> ***Base Offering Circular*** - Umbrella document that covers all MBS/PCs and contains

> general information about pools issued during its effective period, including, but not limited to, the nature of the guarantee, yield considerations, prepayment risk and the mortgage purchase programs.
>
> ***Offering Circular Supplements*** - System generated disclosure document for each MBS/PC created that contains statistical information about the loans specific to a particular pool.

Because the bulk of the participants' rights and responsibilities are set forth in the guides, the Enterprises' transactions are largely standardized. The Enterprises achieve efficiency and cost savings in executing transactions through use of a consistent contractual framework across large securitization transaction volumes, while retaining a degree of flexibility as market conditions and requirements change. During the housing boom, the rules embodied in these guides, and the actual practices followed, had a number of costly deficiencies, which the Conservatorships have made substantial progress in rectifying.

Ginnie Mae Contractual Framework

The current legal document framework used by Ginnie Mae consists of a guide that specifies the requirements for pooling government-backed mortgage loans (primarily loans insured by FHA, VA and two other agencies), issuing MBS backed by such pools and servicing the loans, and a guarantee agreement under which the issuer agrees to comply with the requirements of the guide.

The primary document is a standard Guarantee Agreement between the issuer (a Ginnie Mae approved lender) and Ginnie Mae. Through this document, the issuer assigns all rights, title and interest in the collateral loans in return for Ginnie Mae's guarantee of the securities issued on these loans. The parties also agree that the issuer has the right and obligation to service the portfolio loans while in good standing with Ginnie Mae. This includes holding legal title, making all advances, filing claims and absorbing losses suffered on particular loans. The issuer is not the agent of Ginnie Mae.

Together, the guide and the guarantee agreement are the equivalent of a Private Label PSA and its related mortgage loan purchase agreement. A brief description of the key Ginnie Mae documents includes:

> ***Guarantee Agreement*** - Issuer agrees to comply with the requirements of the guide and Ginnie Mae agrees to guarantee the securities.

Ginnie Mae MBS Guide – Contains instructions to participants regarding issuance, reporting, advances, repurchase, etc. The guide also incorporates the standard form agreements, reporting formats, etc. to be used by issuers. This also includes the guidelines for pooling the mortgage loans and issuing the securities, including the representations and warranties concerning the issuer and the mortgage loans, and requires the issuer (or servicer engaged by it) to service the mortgage loans in accordance with the rules, regulations and guides, if any, of FHA, VA or Rural Development (RD), as applicable.

Custodial Agreement - Identifies the document custodian that the issuer has selected for the pool of loans backing the securities.

Prospectus - Disclosure document for the MBS created containing statistical information about the pool of loans backing the MBS, the nature of the guarantee, and Ginnie Mae's MBS program.

The documents described above are generally standardized, with almost all of the responsibilities of the issuer and the custodian responsibilities being contained in the guide and the responsibilities of the servicer being dictated by the rules, regulations and other guidance of the primary government insurer or guarantor (FHA/VA). This consistent and standardized contractual framework allows issuers to efficiently issue a large volume of Ginnie Mae guaranteed MBS.

Private Label PSAs

The typical Private Label PSA is created on a highly customized basis for each MBS transaction. The PSA sets out the structure of the securities (the number of classes and the right of each class to receive principal and interest payments), as well as the rights and obligations of the seller, the servicer, the trustee, the custodian, the investors and any guarantor or insurer of any of the securities. A separate mortgage loan purchase agreement sets out the general terms of the loans sold by the seller into the securitization trust.

The lack of standardization in the many versions of Private Label PSAs produced divergent business practices that led to ambiguity in interpretation and placed different market participants (i.e., sellers, borrowers, servicers, trustees, senior investors and subordinate investors) at direct odds with each other. In some cases, borrowers in similar circumstances were treated very differently depending on whether their respective PSA permitted a broad or narrow range of loss mitigation alternatives to foreclosure. In other cases, investors were also affected by nonstandardized loan representations and warranties and ineffective mechanisms for enforcing remedies for breaches of representations and warranties. Other issues associated with non-standard PSAs included vague and ambiguous mechanisms for exercising voting rights, the inability to identify and communicate with other investors when securities were held through intermediaries, and lack of information about the performance of mortgage loans in the securitization.

A comparison of the Enterprise, Ginnie Mae and Private Label legal frameworks is provided in Table 1 below.

Table 1: Relationships among FNM, FRE, Ginnie Mae and Private Label Documents

3) Proposed Framework for a New Securitization Infrastructure

The proposed framework contains certain key principles critical to the success of a functional secondary mortgage market. These include promoting liquidity, attracting private capital, benefiting borrowers and operating flexibly and efficiently, while minimizing market disruption during transition.

This framework focuses on functions for which greater standardization would benefit the overall market since these functions are repeated across the industry. The goal is to offer benefits to the broader housing finance market, while not limiting market choices or valuable independent innovations.

The functions highlighted in Figure 3 could be accommodated via the securitization platform through standardized processing, and possibly offered to the market as a form of utility:

Figure 3: New Platform Functions

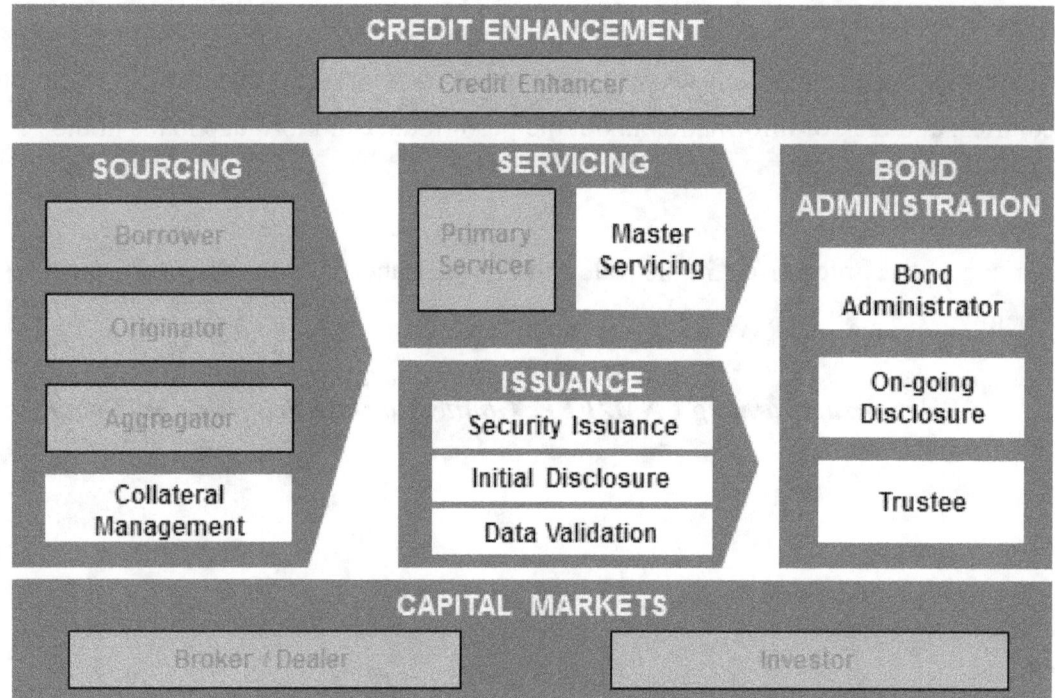

- Collateral management, specifically centralized note tracking.
- Master servicing within the overall servicing related functions, including asset and cash management, standardized interfaces to servicers, guarantors, and aggregators, servicing metrics, data validation and reporting.
- Issuance, including eligibility rules, data quality standards, pool delivery, settlement and disclosure.
- Data validation (servicing and issuance) with the securitization platform storing loan level, pool level, and bond level data to improve data integrity and advance transparency and efficiency in the securitization market.
- Bond administration, including standardized investor and third party disclosures, bond processing, principal and interest distributions, securities monitoring, portfolio reporting and role of Trustee.

In addition to the key functions outlined above, greater consistency as to key contractual features will provide a more stable, liquid and efficient secondary market. That is why another function proposed here is the creation of standardized documents, including a new model PSA that incorporates a robust selling and servicing guide as a way to achieve greater consistency and efficiency in the housing finance market.

A) Proposed Platform

As FHFA stated in the Enterprises' 2012 Conservatorship Scorecards, the Enterprises need to "Develop and finalize a plan by December 31, 2012 for the design and build of a single securitization platform that can serve both Enterprises and a post-conservatorship market with multiple future issuers." The existing infrastructures pose substantial challenges in their ability to adapt to market changes in program, disclosure, or servicing standards, to issue securities that attract private capital, to create full transparency and aggregation of data, and to lower the barriers to entry for new issuers, guarantors or other market entrants.

The following sections describe enhancements and new capabilities that the proposed platform should include.

Credit Risk Distribution

An additional goal of the platform is to facilitate sharing of credit risk much more widely than is currently common, so that the conservatorships have less risk and the private sector more. The infrastructure proposed in this paper is designed to be flexible to accommodate multiple future states of housing finance, thus enabling policy makers to choose housing finance systems in the future that could be far less dependent on government involvement in assuming credit risk.

The envisioned platform would bundle mortgages into any of an array of securities structures and provide all the operational support to process and track the payments from borrowers through to the investors from the time a security is created until its ultimate payoff.

The platform must maintain existing secondary market liquidity, while also enabling the entry and participation of private capital. This means, for example, that the platform should be able to support the current TBA market and securities across a range of fixed and adjustable rates. Consistent with this, the platform should include the high level of automation necessary to process the current volume of industry issuance – more than $100 billion per month.

The platform could also support the distribution of credit risk to the private sector through various credit risk sharing arrangements. For example, the platform could support securities guaranteed by either government or private sector entities, where most or much of the risk of individual loan defaults may first be absorbed by other private sector credit enhancers. Additionally, it could support credit structured securities where various classes of securities holders agree to receive cash flows based on contractual distribution rules. In a credit structured security, senior bonds receive cash flows first, with subordinate bonds absorbing the first credit losses.

Privately guaranteed securities could be similar in nature to the guarantee provided by the Enterprises today but may be different in the future. There may be multiple guarantors assuming credit risk at either the loan level or the security level. The goal of the platform is to be flexible enough to support all potential options and help bring transparency to investors. In addition, the platform could facilitate the return of private capital by supporting various options for credit investors to participate in the market.

Proposed Scope and Functionality

The housing finance lifecycle, shown in Figure 4 below, frames the scope and functions that a platform would serve, and how it would benefit the industry and the housing finance system:

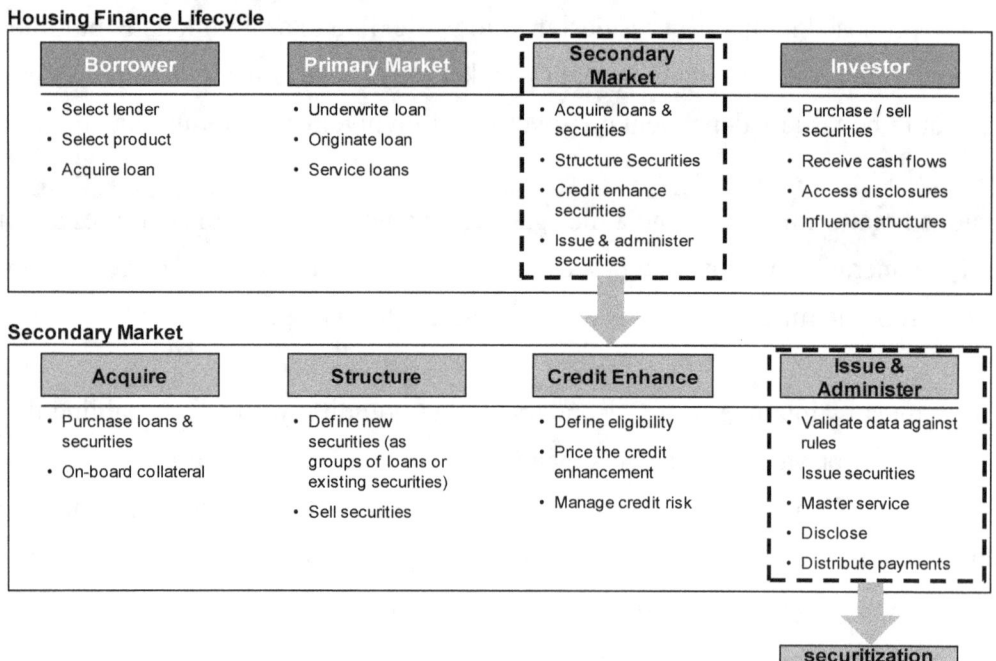

Figure 4: Scope and functions of the platform

Currently, borrowers obtain loans from the primary market, which underwrites, originates, and services mortgages. The primary market sells loans into the secondary market, which: a) acquires loans; b) pools them into securities; c) credit enhances the securities (via subordination structures, private insurance or a government guarantee); and d) issues the securities into the investor marketplace and administers them. At a minimum, this final phase of the housing finance lifecycle can be transformed into an automated securitization platform that could serve both the Enterprises and the wider securitization market of the future.

Specifically, the platform could provide a discrete set of services both at the time of securities issuance, and on an ongoing (typically monthly) basis in support of principal and interest payments to investors. In doing so, it could act under a standard set of operating requirements as an appointed agent for the Security Trustee.

While the platform's proposed design should have the flexibility to increase service offerings based on industry demand and continued evolution of housing finance standards, the initial core services proposed in this paper are intentionally selected as foundational due to their place within the housing finance lifecycle. The initial core services of the proposed platform have the following characteristics:

- The identified services are standard services that lend themselves to straight-through, highly automated processing of large volumes with limited manual intervention.
- As an integrated offering, the identified services accommodate setting and adjusting market standards, and assists market and data transparency.
- The identified services are rules-driven and can readily adapt to changes in market standards and policy – consistent with the imperative that the platform must be able to accommodate and implement future policy decisions about the Enterprises.
- The identified services have the flexibility to serve many industry models.
- The identified services enable the private sector to continue to drive security selection, loan pooling, loan underwriting and other functions not currently performed by the Enterprises.

As shown in Figure 5 below, the platform scope would include the issuance of securities as requested by a user, the monthly master servicing of loans while in the securities, the payment of monies to securities investors, and the tracking and disclosure of securities balances, payments and underlying loan performance data.

Figure 5: Proposed standard services

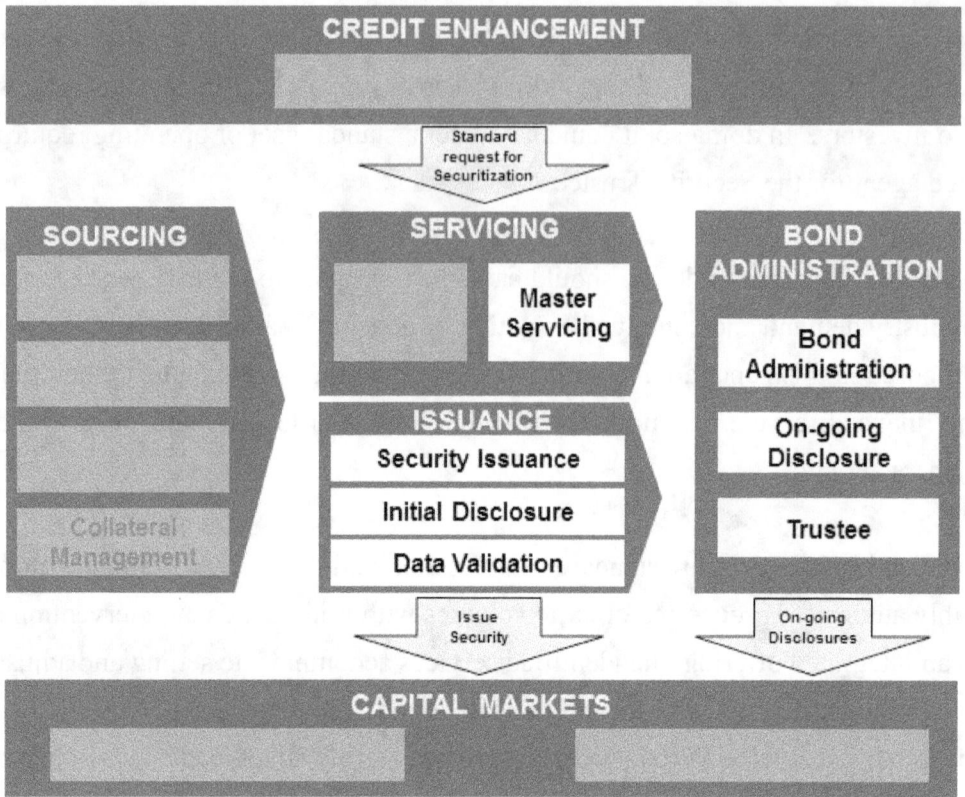

As shown in Figure 6 below, the primary at-issuance services the platform would perform include:

Data validation

The platform data validation service would verify that the request as submitted conforms to agreed-upon standards, and the data format for both loans and securities is correct and complete. Notification would be provided back to the requestor of the acceptance or rejection of the request, along with details on specific rule violations so that deficiencies can be efficiently corrected and requests resubmitted.

Issuance

The platform issuance service, as proposed, would accept the validated request and register the security with the appropriate agent, Federal Reserve (FED) or Depository Trust and Clearing Corporation (DTCC). On the security settlement date, the platform would transfer the security to its initial owner and remit cash proceeds to the issuer according to the instructions provided with the issuance request. The platform would validate that settlement occurred, and provide confirmation back to the issuer. The underlying loan information would be transferred to the Master Servicing service to initiate the master servicing process.

Successful implementation of the proposed PSA framework would leverage the ongoing alignment between the Enterprises of certain business practices through the creation of one set of shared guides and legal agreements. FHFA and the Enterprises have undertaken a number of initiatives to address standardization and alignment of business practices, including:

<u>The Uniform Mortgage Data Program</u> was designed to improve the consistency, quality, and uniformity of data collected at the beginning of the lending process. Developing standard terms, definitions, and data reporting protocols will decrease costs for originators and reduce repurchase risk. It will allow new entrants to use industry standards rather than having to develop their own proprietary data systems to compete with other systems already in the market. Common data definitions, electronic data capture, and standardized data protocols will improve efficiency, lower costs and enhance risk monitoring. Standardizing data will be a key building block of housing finance reform. A standardized purchase data set was implemented during the summer of 2012. Uniform mortgage servicing data set foundation is targeted to be available to key stakeholders for feedback in 2013.

<u>The Servicing Alignment Initiative</u> produced a single, consistent set of protocols for servicing Enterprise mortgages from the moment they first become delinquent. The initiative responded to concerns regarding the servicing of delinquent mortgages, simplifying the rules for mortgage servicers with a uniform set of procedures to follow whether a mortgage is owned by Fannie Mae or Freddie Mac. The first phase of this initiative was implemented in 2012 and could serve as the basis for national mortgage servicing standards, and lay the groundwork for how default servicing should be performed and the compensation for those services.

<u>The Joint Servicing Compensation Initiative</u> considered alternatives for future mortgage servicing compensation for single-family mortgage loans. The broad goals of the initiative were to consider changes to the servicing compensation structure that would improve competition in the market for mortgage servicing and be replicable across any form of housing finance reform. Considering the most appropriate form of servicing compensation will be an important component of the housing finance system of the future.

<u>The Loan-Level Disclosure Initiative</u> will produce loan-level investor disclosures on Enterprise MBS and PCs, both at the time of origination and throughout a security's life.

In addition, the proposed PSA framework would be used to create the credit structure (*e.g.*, senior/sub structures), provide for credit enhancement, if applicable, or provide for any additional provisions the private market may require. As in the case of the Enterprises' current structure, this would allow for the program guides to change over time as market practices and policies evolve. An overview of the proposed working framework is provided below:

A model framework for the PSA could enhance the efficiency of the housing finance market by incorporating standardized provisions and best practices. The key elements for private capital to return to the housing finance market hinge on clear rules and standards about: 1) the integrity of mortgage originations in terms of data and seller responsibilities; 2) the adequacy of servicing; 3) servicer compensation; and 4) disclosures to investors. In addition, there are examples of ongoing work at the Enterprises that can be incorporated into the model PSA: 1) alignment and enhancement of the existing policies, practices, and legal documents of the Enterprises; and 2) standardized servicing, disclosure and other practices of the Enterprises.

The proposed PSA framework would leverage the existing structure used by the Enterprises, as shown in Figure 10. The framework would include a short PSA (or PSA supplement) containing lender/seller specific requirements and variances, general trust provisions and incorporate robust program guides which would set out the requirements for underwriting, disclosure, servicing and loan delivery. The guides would set forth the minimum standards for eligibility to use the proposed industry securitization platform, specify the duties and responsibilities of the securitization platform, reflect a compilation of "best practices" and applicable regulatory requirements for servicing and the other transaction participants, and address certain shortcomings of the Private Label PSA (some of which were discussed earlier).

Figure 10: Proposed PSA Framework

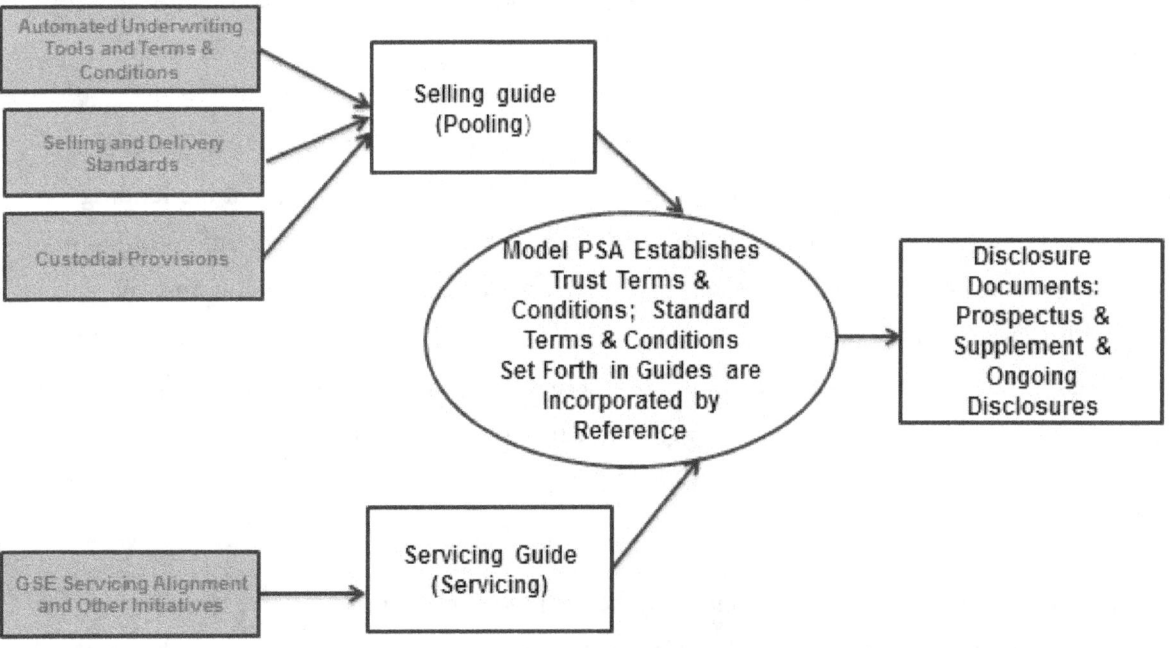

This, in conjunction with the proposed PSA framework, could improve service to borrowers, reduce financial risk to servicers, and provide flexibility and data for guarantors to better manage non-performing loans. The Uniform Mortgage Servicing Dataset Initiative will make standard servicing interactions (such as servicing transfers, loan removals from securities, etc.) consistent and transparent across the industry.

3) Disclosures to Investors

Improved disclosure with better information would enable investors to efficiently measure and price mortgage credit risk, which is a necessary component of enhancing opportunities for private capital participation. The platform would be capable of disclosing the full transparency of information made available through the ULDD, and through the enhanced automation of monthly loan reporting process discussed above. Data would be made available both in a streamlined electronic format for consumption by third party data providers, as well as in a user-accessible web-based portal allowing for investor-customized views and reporting. Additionally, by employing event-based data capture and processing, the platform could provide increased consistency, frequency, and quality of data both at the time of origination and throughout a security's lifecycle.

4) Loan and Security Reporting to Issuers/Guarantors

Updated loan and security positions, along with other data that issuers and guarantors require to do their business (accounting, tracking, etc.) would be provided in a secure, standard data format to each issuer for their securities. The Uniform Mortgage Data Program can be extended to maintain standard terms, definitions, and data reporting protocols for all data reported back to Issuers.

Applying these standards and processes across the entire spectrum of the securitization chain would ensure consistency, quality, and uniformity of data collected throughout the lending process. Common data definitions, electronic data capture, and standardized data protocols would improve efficiency, lower costs and enhance risk monitoring. Extending already developed standard terms, definitions, and industry data reporting protocols, where feasible, would decrease costs for issuers/guarantors to interact with the platform, and allow new entrants to use industry standards rather than having to develop proprietary interfaces.

B) Proposed PSA Framework

For all the importance of a suitable platform, the proposed integrated infrastructure cannot function without the appropriate legal agreements, rules and allocations of responsibilities, including a framework for an effective contractual PSA.

Figure 9: Standard requests and reports

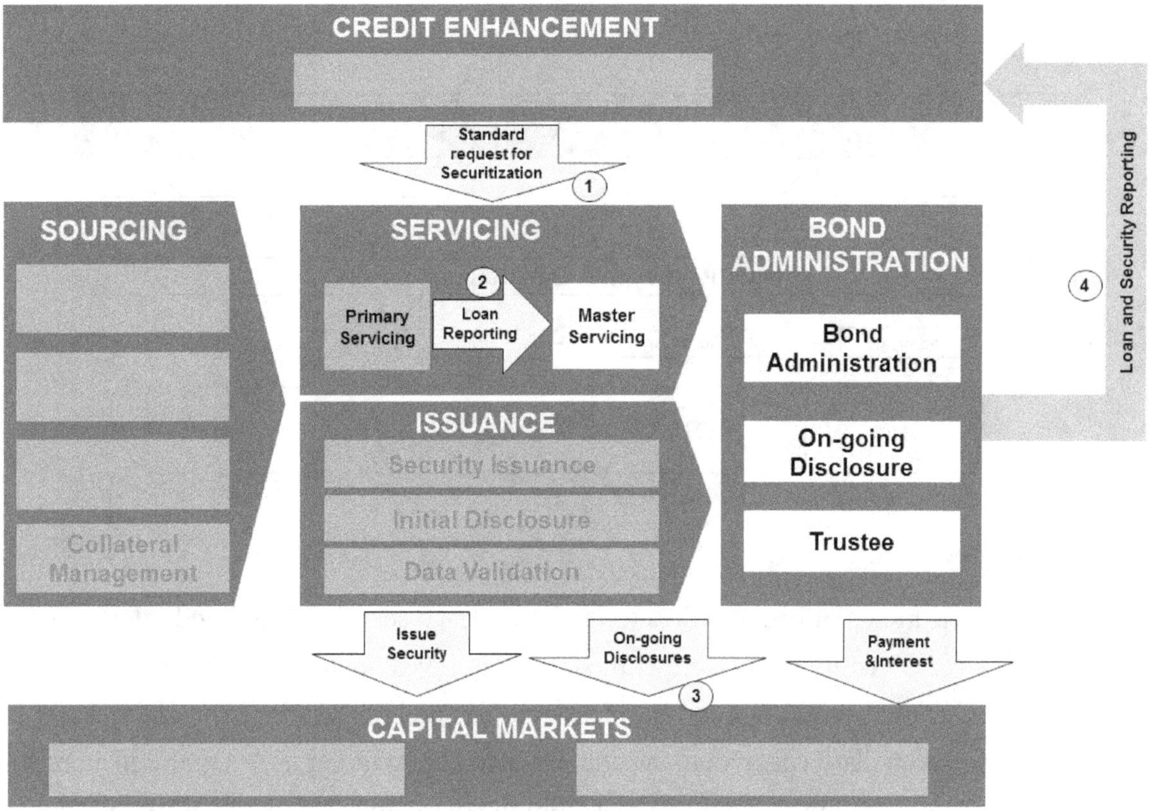

These proposed interactions build on and extend existing industry open standards to advance transparency and level the playing field. Figure 9 illustrates the interactions that will be discussed below.

1) Standard Requests for Securitization

Under previous FHFA guidance, the Enterprises are transitioning their single-family loan delivery data formats to a ULDD that leverages the industry-recognized MISMO Version 3.0 standard. Through this joint work, common usage for the majority of the loan delivery data elements is being established, also allowing for a richer set of investor disclosures. The platform would leverage and where needed expand upon this model, allowing the primary market to deliver bundles of mortgages into any of an array of securities structures, including those that support PLS and other innovative credit transfer facilities.

2) Loan Reports from Primary Servicers

The platform would provide operational support to process and track the payments from borrowers through to the investors, by leveraging the Uniform Mortgage Servicing Dataset Initiative to define a standard servicing data dictionary and standards-based data exchange.

Figure 8: Design principles

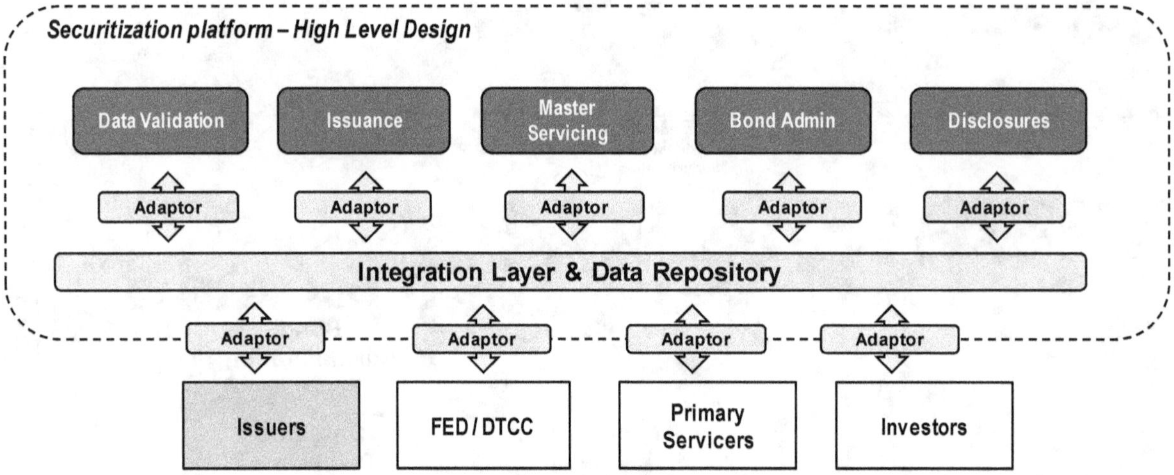

Platform Interoperability

A common securitization platform requires a standards-based set of well-defined interfaces for interactions between all entities involved with connecting investors to homeowners. The platform services would have a common business and data architecture to drive interoperability, both internally between platform components, and externally, creating an open architecture for all these elements, to facilitate entry to and exit from the marketplace and an ability to adapt to emerging technologies.

The platform's open architecture tenet would be realized through a service integration approach that publishes and supports connectivity standards – agnostic to any issuer/Enterprise, servicer, agent, or other counterparty. The goal of service integration is to provide market participants with the proper support to adjust to the new structure in order to minimize disruptions and uncertainty. Standard interfaces would frame all platform data exchanges – both into and out of the platform. The platform's standard inputs could include requests for issuance, periodic servicer loan reports, and unscheduled requests such as non-performing loan removal. Standard outputs could include issued securities and prospectuses, disclosure reporting to investors, loan and security activity reports, and exception processing information.

Design Principles and Technical Approach

The platform should adhere to clearly defined design principles in order to provide a sound foundation on which to rebuild the country's secondary mortgage market, and must maintain flexibility on several levels. Specifically, it should be adaptable to policy change, able to standardize interfaces with participants and remain configurable in light of future standards and emerging technologies. These are important high-level principles expressing the proposed platform's technical approach.

But there a handful of other, more specific design principles that will guide how the platform is designed and built. We review them below and depict them in Figure 8.

- Open architecture – Standard external interfaces would be established for efficient interoperability with multiple Issuers/Enterprises. The platform would leverage existing industry data standards (e.g. MISMO, Uniform Loan Delivery Dataset (ULDD), Uniform Mortgage Data Program, etc.).

- Functional modularity – Platform internal components would communicate via standard interfaces to ensure that modifying, configuring, replacing, or adding new functional modules can be accomplished with minimal impact across the platform.

- Scalability – Integration architecture would be employed based on standard technologies with proven scale in financial services and multiple industries, to ensure accommodation of growth demands and increased throughput.

- Data transparency – Data architecture would be developed that provides data traceability and accessibility via common data infrastructure and data standards.

  Straight-through processing and event automation – Event-driven system architecture would be incorporated that minimizes manual intervention to drive efficient operations and performance, and allows for capture of operational and market metrics centrally and at a granular data level.

Bond administration would support a wide spectrum of re-securitizations; single class security backed by existing single class securitizes (both first level securitizations and existing re-securitizations); multiclass securities backed by existing single class securities; multiclass securities backed by existing multiclass securities; and multiclass securities backed by whole loans. Multiclass securities include REMIC (Real Estate Mortgage Investment Conduits), SMBS (Stripped Mortgage Backed Securities) and Grantor Trust structures. The platform should have the ability to support the use of securities from various issuers as collateral for re-securitizations. Tax reporting for the securities, either single class or multi-class, would be supported by the platform.

The platform would collect funds due investors on the collateral (loans from master servicing or existing securities) and invest the funds in eligible investments. Payment instructions would be provided to the paying agent (FED, DTCC or physical certificates) for appropriate fund distribution. The platform could perform these and any other required activities as directed by the Trust or other governing security documents.

Figure 7 highlights these proposed platform services, responsible for distributing payments to investors and disclosing updates to loans and securities:

Figure 7: Proposed on-going payment services

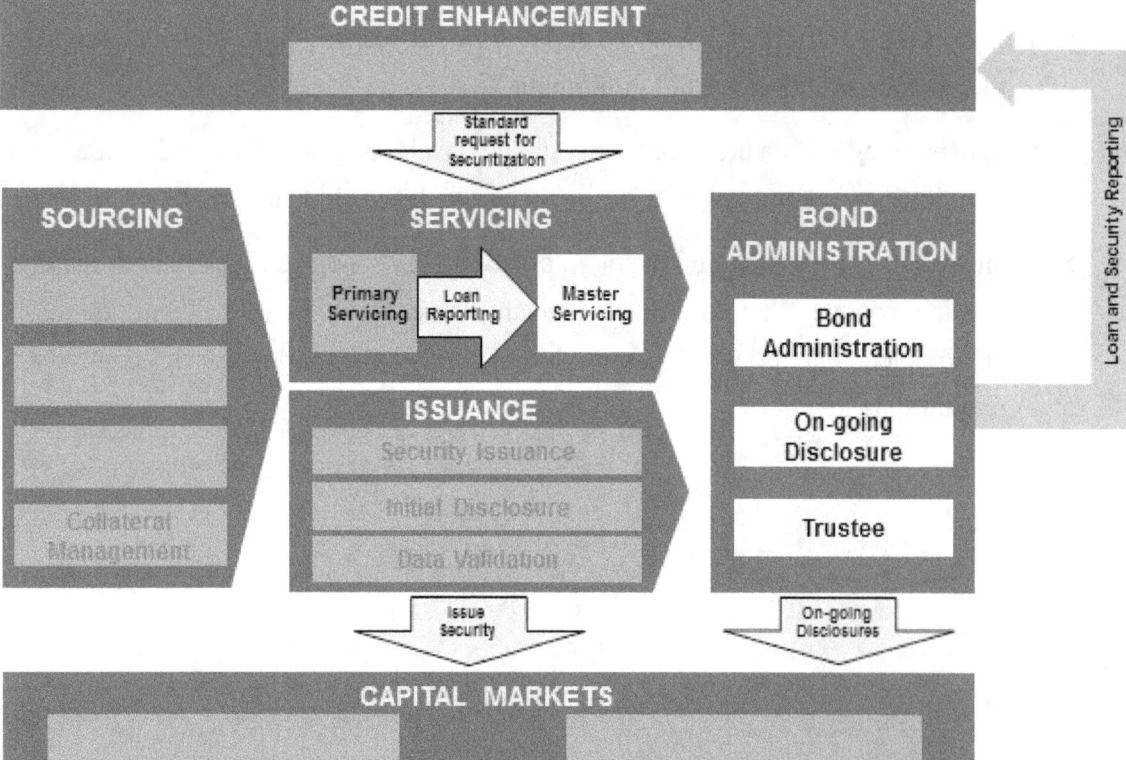

management activities as directed by a trust or other governing security documents. This includes collecting and processing primary servicer loan activity and verifying that principal and interest payments are correct for each reporting cycle.

Some of the services provided by the platform would include: performance of security balance roll up from loan balances at the end of each reporting cycle, and transmission of data to the bond administration function as discussed below. Master servicing in the platform would handle varying cycles and reporting/remitting cut-off dates to support various security programs while working with servicers, sub-servicers, interim servicers and special servicers.

Primary servicers could provide investor reporting and cash directly to the platform or via other parties, with standardized reporting and remitting dates. This would increase the speed and efficiency of reconciliations and reporting to downstream credit enhancers and investors. The platform could also support servicer compensation based on either a negotiated fee for service or a flat fee strip amount to provide flexibility to implement future changes to servicer compensation.

On an as-required basis, the platform would be responsible for processing requests to remove loans from securities, make approved modifications to loans, transfer primary servicing or ownership interests and provide delinquency reporting on non-performing loans. These actions would be taken at the direction of the issuer, the trustee, or in accordance with governing documents and delegations.

The platform could monitor and direct document custody, and monitor primary servicer performance for adherence to standards as well as all other compliance directives requested by the trustee or other governing documents. It could have the ability to provide updated loan and security positions.

<u>Bond Administration</u>
Bond administration would be responsible for calculating investor payment factors and making data available to the disclosure function for ongoing investor reporting for each payment cycle. Bond administration would support both first level securitizations (securities backed directly by loans) and second level re-securitizations (securities backed by existing securities). Bond administration would also ensure payments to investors and other parties are managed in a timely manner.

The security data would also be transferred to the disclosure service.

Disclosures

Disclosure covers the process whereby attributes describing a security and underlying loans or pools are published to the marketplace in a timely manner. Preliminary disclosure occurs before the security settles in order to alert the market to a pending security's fundamental characteristics. On settlement date, the platform would publish the final disclosure, which includes detailed information describing the final loan pool and security structure.

On-going disclosure occurs monthly, or when relevant changes occur to the pool or underlying loans. Disclosure documents proposed to be published would include the prospectus supplements and supplemental oversight documents. Disclosure information would be published by the platform on the Internet and possibly in other forms.

Figure 6: Proposed at issuance services

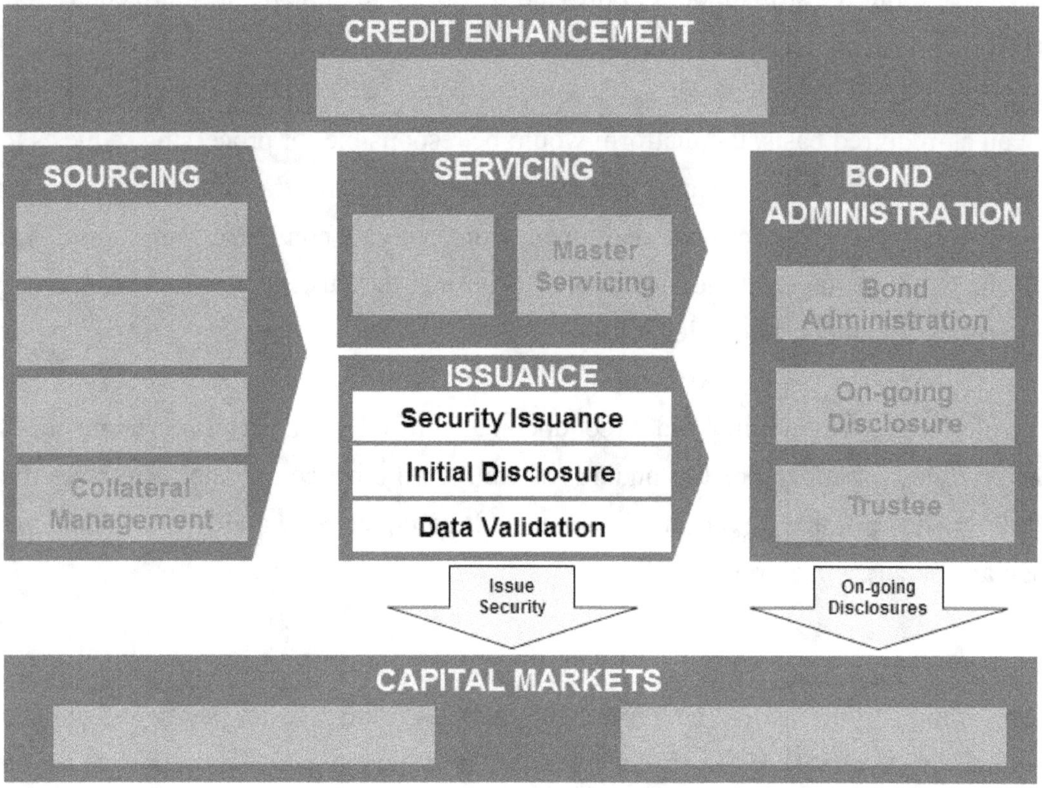

The primary ongoing payment services the platform as proposed would perform include:

Master Servicing

The master servicing functions performed by the platform include asset and cash

Figure 5: Proposed standard services

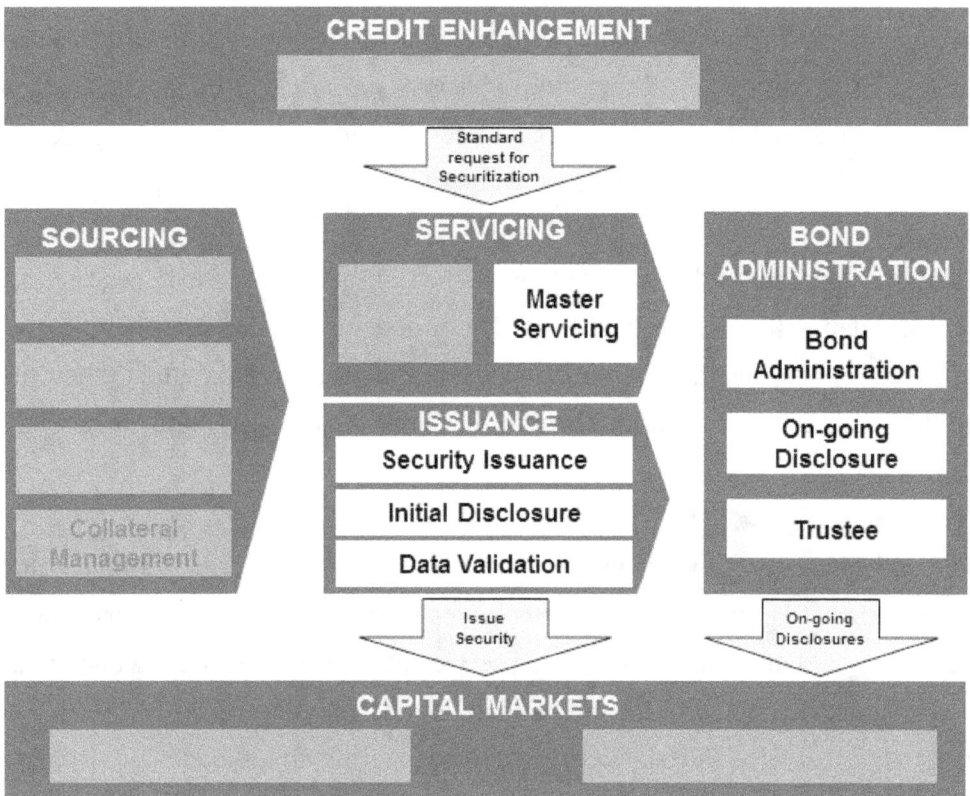

As shown in Figure 6 below, the primary at-issuance services the platform would perform include:

Data validation
The platform data validation service would verify that the request as submitted conforms to agreed-upon standards, and the data format for both loans and securities is correct and complete. Notification would be provided back to the requestor of the acceptance or rejection of the request, along with details on specific rule violations so that deficiencies can be efficiently corrected and requests resubmitted.

Issuance
The platform issuance service, as proposed, would accept the validated request and register the security with the appropriate agent, Federal Reserve (FED) or Depository Trust and Clearing Corporation (DTCC). On the security settlement date, the platform would transfer the security to its initial owner and remit cash proceeds to the issuer according to the instructions provided with the issuance request. The platform would validate that settlement occurred, and provide confirmation back to the issuer. The underlying loan information would be transferred to the Master Servicing service to initiate the master servicing process.

both the Enterprises and the wider securitization market of the future.

Specifically, the platform could provide a discrete set of services both at the time of securities issuance, and on an ongoing (typically monthly) basis in support of principal and interest payments to investors. In doing so, it could act under a standard set of operating requirements as an appointed agent for the Security Trustee.

While the platform's proposed design should have the flexibility to increase service offerings based on industry demand and continued evolution of housing finance standards, the initial core services proposed in this paper are intentionally selected as foundational due to their place within the housing finance lifecycle. The initial core services of the proposed platform have the following characteristics:

- The identified services are standard services that lend themselves to straight-through, highly automated processing of large volumes with limited manual intervention.
- As an integrated offering, the identified services accommodate setting and adjusting market standards, and assists market and data transparency.
- The identified services are rules-driven and can readily adapt to changes in market standards and policy – consistent with the imperative that the platform must be able to accommodate and implement future policy decisions about the Enterprises.
- The identified services have the flexibility to serve many industry models.
- The identified services enable the private sector to continue to drive security selection, loan pooling, loan underwriting and other functions not currently performed by the Enterprises.

As shown in Figure 5 below, the platform scope would include the issuance of securities as requested by a user, the monthly master servicing of loans while in the securities, the payment of monies to securities investors, and the tracking and disclosure of securities balances, payments and underlying loan performance data.

Improving MBS and PC disclosures will help establish consistency and quality of data. With better information, private investors can efficiently measure and price mortgage credit risk, which will likely be a hallmark of any type of housing refinance reform.

Representation and Warranty – FHFA's recent announcement on the launch of a new representations and warranty (rep and warranty) framework for conventional loans sold or delivered on or after January 1, 2013 is part of a broader set of initiatives to harmonize the Enterprises' seller-servicer contracts. It aims to clarify lenders' repurchase exposure and liability on future deliveries.

FHFA proposes that the Enterprises continue the ongoing improvements to the guides and legal agreements not only to support ongoing efforts to achieve efficiencies, but also to provide the broader private market with more standardized securitization policies and practices to ultimately foster private capital participation in credit risk. The benefits will be realized as the Enterprises move to a common set of documents, thus providing the foundation for the private market to either build upon or use directly.

4) Policy and Regulatory Considerations

Creation of a common securitization platform and a PSA framework should be designed to help regulators and policymakers effectively deal with key policy considerations. The design of the common securitization platform does not assume a continuation of government's role in the mortgage market but would support a government guarantee if the future housing model incorporated one. In addition, the platform would have the flexibility to accept different levels of credit standards and mortgage products for participation giving policymakers the ability to specify any minimum standards or product eligibility.

The platform and PSA framework could help enforce Qualified Mortgage (QM)/Qualified Residential Mortgage (QRM) guidelines, screening for QM/QRM eligibility, and identifying any corresponding risk retention requirements. To the extent that other proposed rules on mortgage origination or servicing become binding regulations, these could serve as tools to help monitor industry compliance. The proposed PSA framework would leverage ongoing Enterprise alignment work in many areas that are important to a functional secondary market. The framework would not only benefit from the ongoing alignment of the Enterprises' standards and practices, but also the proposed PSA framework would create a consistent and uniform platform of best practices and standards for facilitating participation of private capital to the secondary market.

5) Conclusion

The Strategic Plan envisions the building of a securitization infrastructure to supplant the Enterprises' outmoded infrastructures, offer a useful facility to the secondary mortgage market, and facilitate the entry of private capital investment in credit risk. The securitization platform would support the existing securitization business of the Enterprises while in conservatorship. It would conserve taxpayer funds from maintaining and upgrading two parallel infrastructures during their transition to a yet to be determined future state, pending decisions by policy makers. FHFA's intent is to build both a securitization platform and a model PSA, which could improve the efficiency and effectiveness of the secondary mortgage market while preserving policy options. This coordinated effort between FHFA and the Enterprises, with substantial industry input, will continue to facilitate the functioning of the secondary mortgage market while the Enterprises remain in Conservatorship, and provide a valuable tool for policymakers to consider.

This paper has defined the scope of the proposed changes and identified the functions that FHFA believes should be included in the new securitization infrastructure that can support the mortgage finance system. The paper has also described the steps FHFA and the Enterprises are taking, with industry input, to develop new standards for pooling and servicing of loans and for loan data and disclosure requirements that will standardize and improve the process of securitizing mortgages. Aligning the Enterprises with one set of policies, guides, documents, processes and a new securitization platform will create standards and a model for private capital and help facilitate post-Conservatorship outcomes. Building a new securitization infrastructure is likely to be a multi-year effort. Various aspects of securitization that fall under the purview of the industry, regulatory agencies and policymakers will have bearing on the final structures that emerge.

FHFA has required, as part of the Enterprises' 2012 Conservatorship Scorecards, that the Enterprises submit a plan for the securitization platform and propose a model PSA and make recommendations for standard Enterprise trust documentation by December 31, 2012. FHFA seeks public input on the design principles and execution approach discussed in this paper to help inform these efforts. In addition FHFA requests specific input on the following questions to ensure that the final design reflects a full range of industry input.

Questions

FHFA is requesting that all interested parties provide written input on the proposal presented in this paper. Below are specific questions on which FHFA is seeking input. While this effort is not a notice and comment rulemaking subject to the requirements of the Administrative Procedures Act, the purpose is to provide a mechanism for industry input – a critical factor in the acceptance and ultimate success of the initiative. Input on the white paper must be received by December 3, 2012, and should be addressed to: *Federal Housing Finance Agency, Office of Strategic Initiatives, 400 7th Street, S.W., Washington, DC 20024*. Input may also be submitted via email to SecuritizationInfrastructure@fhfa.gov or directly on FHFA's website at the following link: http://www.fhfa.gov/default.aspx?Page=-995&Survey=2. After December 3rd, FHFA plans to post the input on FHFA's website for public review.

1. The proposed securitization platform has four core functions (issuance, disclosure, bond administration and master servicing). Will these core functions provide an efficient and effective foundation for the housing finance system going forward?

2. Are there additional functionalities that should be considered as core functions of the platform? For example, should the platform independently verify or determine the following or rely on an issuer or guarantor:

    a. underwriting and loan eligibility rules?

    b. pooling rules?

3. Will the framework for a model PSA described in this paper provide the foundation for a standardized contractual framework for the housing finance system going forward?

4. Are there additional elements/attributes that should be included in a model PSA? For example,

    a. should the model PSA define when a non-performing loan is required to be purchased out of the trust?

    b. should the model PSA define when a non-performing loan is required to be transferred to a specialty servicer?

5. If the framework for a model PSA is a good contractual foundation, how should compliance with the PSA be monitored in the future?

6. What enhancements to the role of trustee should be considered in order to better attract private capital to the housing finance system?

7. How should document custodial and assignment responsibilities be handled in the housing finance system going forward?

www.ingramcontent.com/pod-product-compliance
Lightning Source LLC
Chambersburg PA
CBHW081811170526
45167CB00008B/3402